MAKE DO AND MEND

MAKE DO AND MEND

Summersdale Publishers Ltd
46 West Street
Chichester
West Sussex
PO19 1RP
UK

www.summersdale.com

Printed and bound in China

ISBN: 978-1-84953-285-3

MAKE DO AND MEND

summersdale

CONTENTS

INTRODUCTION

Make Do and Mend is the perfect accompaniment to these cash-strapped times. Within these pages you will discover that it's not just about making do, it's about getting creative: whether you take a pair of scissors to a favourite old dress that has seen better days and revamp it into a bespoke new outfit, with a tuck here and a new fastening there, or you harvest forgotten produce from the larder to rustle up something delicious and homemade rather than dashing to the shops for a ready-meal.

Being thrifty is about saying no to waste, saving money and enjoying the good things in life on a budget, and this guide with tips on how to live inexpensively will show you how. Interspersed with slogans from ration-era Britain to cheer you on, and sage quotes from the worldly wise, you'll be cutting up those credit cards in no time!

CLOTHING AND FOOTWEAR

Remove winter salt stains from shoes by wiping with a cloth dampened in a vinegar solution. Use one part vinegar to six parts water.

Restore old shoes by rubbing a sliced raw potato onto the leather. Polish them with a cloth and watch them gleam.

Another way to restore the shine on leather shoes is to apply a dash of vegetable oil. Use a damp cloth to remove any dirt, then run a soft cloth with a drop of oil over the surface to (literally) add polish.

Don't throw away a garment because the zip seems stuck fast; rub the metal teeth with a pencil lead – you should now be able to ease it open.

Add a teaspoon of pepper to a colour wash to keep colours bright and prevent runs.

Learn how to darn beloved woollen items when they hole. A fabric shop or haberdashery department will have a range of wools or silks from which to match colours to your garment, as well as needles for sale.

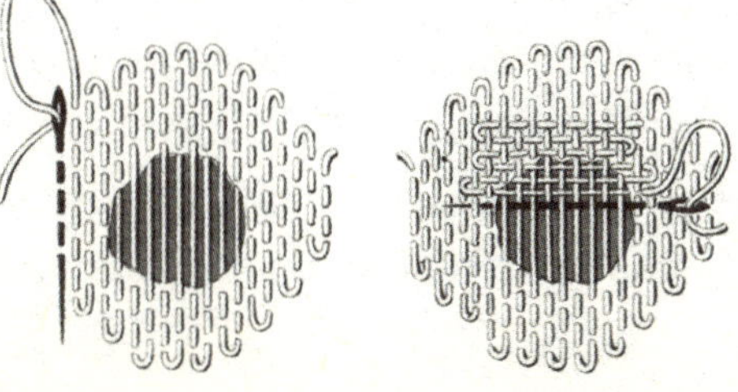

To deter moths naturally, forget chemical-based mothballs; simply make lavender bags to hang amongst clothing – lavender is a natural moth repellent.

To remove dried bloodstains from clothing, dampen the offending area with cold water, rub with a bar of natural soap, create a lather and then work the lather into the fabric. Rinse with cold water. Sometimes the process will have to be repeated, but this is a fail-safe method to restore fabrics to their former glory.

Faded colours? Try rinsing your clothes in water with some vinegar. This helps get rid of the dulling effect of washing powder residue that can build up within the fabric.

Turn garments inside out before washing (especially corduroy). This prevents fading (with items such as denim, black jeans or T-shirts with logos) and also helps keep your clothes fluff-free on the outside.

If you have chewing gum on an item of clothing, place the garment into a plastic bag and in the freezer overnight. You can then scrape off as much gum as possible, rub in a little white wine vinegar and wash as normal.

Look at old knitted jumpers as raw materials for something else. Consider unravelling them and reusing the yarn by knitting or crocheting them into something new.

Most clothing can be reinforced in weak places like elbows, the crutch of trousers, and any other part which bears a lot of strain or gets rubbed. Any lightweight material can be used, thus ensuring garments last longer.

If the front of a blouse has become too tight, place a contrasting piece of fabric along the button band. Or if it has long sleeves, make them short and use the material left over for your button band.

Don’t take the squander bug when you go shopping

World War Two slogan

The safe way to double your money is to fold it over once and put it in your pocket.

Frank McKinney Hubbard

For a blouse which is hardly ever worn because it is too short in the waist, working its way out of the top of the skirt, a deep band of near-matching fabric can be added all round to the hem which once tucked in will be barely noticeable.

Place a few needles, pins and thread into a matchbox for an instant sewing kit.

Prevent camisoles and sundresses slipping off hangers by wrapping the hanger ends with rubber bands.

A well-worn cardigan can be restored to form by lightly running a pumice stone across the surface to lift off any unsightly bobbles.

To eliminate lipstick from an item of clothing, saturate the spot with hairspray, leave it for ten minutes, then dab with a damp cloth or sponge to remove. Wash as usual to clean out any residual stain and spray.

Stop tights from laddering once holed by dabbing the area with a touch of nail varnish.

A plain, boring old T-shirt can be brightened up with fabric paints, buttons, ribbon or lace.

If clothes are no longer wearable, cut them up and use them for rags and dishcloths, which can be used for washing-up, wiping down surfaces or even cleaning the car.

To replenish an umbrella's waterproofing, spray on some cheap hairspray to seal it again.

If you have a pair of tall boots and don't want to pay for expensive boot supports, place an empty wine bottle in each boot – it'll do just the same job.

PERSONAL HYGIENE

Forget expensive denture cleanser, instead soak dentures in vinegar for about 15 minutes, then brush thoroughly for shiny bright whiteness, and rinse in water before use.

Sprinkle salt into sweaty trainers or summer shoes – leave overnight then shake out the residue – fresher footwear for the forthcoming day.

Relieve the itch from mosquito or midge bites by soaking the nibbled area in salt water, then dabbing dry and coating with olive or vegetable oil.

Give your hair a natural shine without using expensive conditioners: after washing rinse in unsweetened tea.

Relieve tired eyes by soaking two teabags in warm water and placing them over closed eyes for twenty minutes – a natural remedy for reducing puffiness.

You don't need to spend money on an expensive pedicure; rub feet with body lotion and wear socks to bed – the next day your feet will be as soft as soft can be.

Take a leaf out of Cleopatra's book and prepare yourself a milk bath. Milk has magical properties that help to cleanse, moisturise and tone. Mix 150 ml of powdered milk with a few drops of essential oil, add 50 g of ground almonds and 100 g of porridge oats and pour into a muslin bag (or a recycled nylon stocking or tight). Fill a bath with warm water, immerse the bag and gently swill the water around until it turns cloudy. Lower yourself into the tub and enjoy a relaxing and rejuvenating soak.

A mixture of lemon juice and vinegar can be rubbed in as a toenail fungicide.

If you run out of antiperspirant deodorant, raid your kitchen cupboard. Wipe alcohol on your skin to eliminate bacteria and then apply corn starch. This is an effective solution to ward off unwanted bodily odours.

Mix one tablespoon of apple cider vinegar with one cup of warm water, and apply the vinegar rinse after shampooing. This natural product removes the dulling effect from the build-up of hair styling products and may be used once or twice a week.

Sprinkle a pinch of sugar over a burned tongue to ease the pain.

For hair that has become very dry, massage mayonnaise into your hair. Wrap the hair in plastic or put on a shower cap, and wait. Leave in for an hour or more for extremely damaged hair. Wash out with a mild shampoo until all of the mayonnaise is removed and condition as normal.

Grate fresh coconut flesh and mix with coconut milk, then apply this mixture to your skin for a glowing anti-ageing effect.

Camomile tea can help soothe the pain of mouth ulcers. Cool the tea with the teabag still in, and swish the liquid around the mouth before swallowing. If done every few hours it is thought to relieve inflammation.

Perfect solutions of our difficulties are not to be looked for in an imperfect world.

Winston Churchill

We make ourselves rich by making our wants few.

Henry David Thoreau

To heal a verruca, tape the inside of the peel from an overripe banana to the verruca before going to bed. Repeat every night until the verruca is gone. The sticky substance inside the peel is antiviral.

To prevent discolouration of the teeth, chew a piece of sugarless gum after drinking tea or coffee. This causes an increase in saliva production, helping to wash away the liquids before they have a chance to stain the teeth.

To clear cold sores, blend tea tree oil with an equal amount of olive oil and use a cotton bud to apply two or three times a day.

Add sugar to your usual soap and lather into your face for a couple of minutes. The gentle exfoliating action of the sugar acts as an excellent cleanser, leaving skin soft and clean. Rinse face thoroughly with cool water afterwards.

Make your own cleansing milk by adding some chopped peppermint leaves to a bowl of milk. Leave to infuse overnight in the fridge. The next day, strain the mixture into a bottle, keep refrigerated, and the peppermint cleansing milk is now ready to use.

Instead of buying expensive exfoliators, use sea salt to remove dry and flaky skin. Simply wet skin first then rub in a handful of salt and rinse off.

Once a week, use a natural honey face mask for softer skin and to cleanse pores. Honey is antibacterial and the best type to use is raw honey, which usually has a sugary texture and doesn't drip like processed honey.

Apply thin slices of potato to the eyes for ten minutes to lighten the skin and fade dark circles.

To avoid wasting toothpaste, place a clothes peg on the bottom of the tube and wind the tube over it.

Add water to shampoo and conditioner to make it go further – this won't reduce their effectiveness.

To remove unpleasant odours, strike a match, or light a candle and allow it to burn for a few seconds.

Apply hand cream before putting on rubber gloves to do the washing-up. The heat from the water will help the cream soak into your hands and leave them nice and soft.

HOUSEHOLD CLEANING

Dispense with harmful and expensive chemical fly spray and try filling an old water pistol with vinegar to squirt at the pesky insects for the same results.

Make brooms last longer by soaking bristles in a bucket of hot, salty water for about half an hour. Leave to dry and get sweeping.

Although it may seem like a waste of the good stuff, remove red wine spillages on fabrics (clothes or carpet) by dropping white wine onto the offending stain. Take a dry cloth to soak up the liquid and, hey presto, the stain is removed.

Mix a paste of a spoonful of salt and a few drops of water and rub with a soft cloth into watermarks on wood until the ghosts of damp glasses or bottles are exorcised. Buff with a furniture polish to restore the natural sheen.

Make your own furniture polish: grate beeswax into a heatproof container, add turpentine and heat over a bain-marie until the beeswax dissolves. Add a few drops of natural oil, such as lavender. Once cooled, apply to furniture with a soft cloth and buff to a sheen.

Restore your favourite teacup to its former glory by rubbing salt into stubborn stains with a sponge. Rinse, smile and put the kettle on for a fresh brew.

If you have a budding muralist daubing wax crayon on painted white walls, remove the offending artwork by gently rubbing with a sponge and toothpaste – perfect results every time.

Add a cup of bicarbonate of soda to your washing machine drum and run a hot wash cycle on a regular basis to get rid of bad smells and washing machine detergent build-up. This method can prolong the life of your washing machine.

Home is the place where, no matter where you're sitting, you're looking at something you should be doing.

Anonymous

Housework can kill you if done right.

Erma Bombeck

Pour cat litter or washing powder into the bin to soak up leaking liquids. It also prevents mould growth and keeps the bin smelling fresh.

Before clearing snow off a driveway, liberally spray both sides of a plastic or metal shovel with cooking spray. The ice will slide right off the oily surface, making snow removal so much easier.

Apply a dab of baby oil to a cotton cloth and use it to shine anything chrome, from taps to hubcaps.

For unwanted marks made by permanent marker pen, apply a little rubbing alcohol to the mark with a paper towel. The alcohol should dissolve the mark from the permanent marker. If unsuccessful, soak an area of the paper towel with the rubbing alcohol and lay it on the affected area. Allow to set for a few minutes while it dissolves the mark on the area.

To remove wax from carpeting, use an ice cube to encourage the wax to become cold and hard. Next use a soft-edged plastic spatula or a credit card to scrape up as much of the wax as you can. Place some paper towels over the affected area, turn on the iron to a low-heat setting, and place it on the towels. As the wax softens up because of the heat, the paper towels will become saturated. Lift up the iron to make sure that the wax has not soaked all the way through so that there is no damage to the iron. Repeat the process until all the wax has been removed.

Toothpaste may be able to help remove rubber stains from the kitchen floor. Scrub toothpaste onto the mark until it fades away and wipe the residue off with a wet paper towel.

There's no need for expensive silver polish. Try rubbing a banana skin on silver for a brilliant shine.

IN THE KITCHEN

Add a pinch of salt to a pint of milk to help it stay fresher for longer.

Prevent cheese from going mouldy by storing it with a few lumps of sugar in an airtight container.

Keep cut flowers blooming for longer – stand them in a vase of water where you have dissolved three spoonfuls of sugar, and two spoonfuls of white vinegar.

Halve a lemon and place inside a fridge to eliminate bad smells. The same principle can be applied to microwaves: place a couple of slices of lemon on a plate and microwave briefly and hey presto! No more bad smells.

Half a lemon placed in a kettle of water and boiled a few times will remove the limescale.

Soak burned-on stains in enamel pans in salt water overnight – boil the liquid the following day and watch the stains disappear.

Compost your vegetable peelings, and the compost made from them can be used when planting your veg plot.

Put candles in the fridge or freezer before lighting them – the coldness prolongs their burning life.

If the kitchen sink is totally blocked, pour some very hot water down the drain, followed by a mixture of hot water and vinegar (about a fifty–fifty mixture). Complete by adding another mixture, this time of fifty–fifty hot water and bleach.

- - - - - - - - - - -

To spruce up a stainless steel sink, pour a few drops of olive oil onto a cloth and rub it all over the sink and fixtures. Then go over it again with a dry cloth to ensure the sink is clean, shiny and free of water spots.

To prevent halved avocados from turning brown, refrigerate them flesh side down in a bowl of water into which you have squeezed some lemon juice. They will keep for several days.

It is best to regularly clean a waste disposal outlet at least once a month. First pour about half a cup of baking soda down the drain. Follow this by slowly pouring half a cup of vinegar down the drain. When the fizzing action has stopped, turn on both the water and the drain to remove whatever is left.

A clear plate
means
A clear conscience

World War Two slogan

A stitch in time saves nine.

Proverb

Spilt food in the microwave can be easier to clean by heating a bowl of water inside until it boils. Remove the water, then clean with a damp cloth and some cleaner. The boiling water releases steam that loosens stuck-on stains and spills.

To remove tomato or pasta sauce stains from clothing, cut a lemon in half and squeeze the juice on the spot. Then, scrub the spot with the rind of the lemon and put into the washing machine and wash as usual.

To remove burnt rice from a saucepan, add about three tablespoons of baking soda to about two cups of water. Pour this mixture into the pot, and then place the pot onto the stove and heat to a gentle boil. Allow the water to boil for about three minutes, and then remove. Scrape the bottom of the pan, and then wash as normal.

Recycle leftover pieces of aluminium foil by using them to scrub off baked-on food from glass dishes or an oven rack. Rub in washing-up liquid with a ball of foil.

Avoid storing potatoes near onions – otherwise they spoil sooner.

To quickly bring refrigerated butter to room temperature, fill a water glass with very hot tap water and let it sit for several seconds to warm the glass. Empty the water and turn the glass upside down over the butter. The butter softens in less than a minute without melting.

To preserve the taste of freshly baked cookies and brownies, place a slice of bread in the storage container. The moisture from the bread keeps the cookies soft.

To prevent raisins or chocolate chips from sinking in cake batter dust them first in flour.

By sowing frugality we reap liberty, a golden harvest.

Agesilaus

The only thing I've been able to figure out about stove cleaning is to move house every couple of years.

P. J. O'Rourke

To lift stubborn food stains like burnt milk in a pan, sprinkle on some baking soda, add enough water to cover, and leave it for a couple of hours.

To remove the smell of garlic or onion on a chopping board, sprinkle it with table salt. Cut a lemon or lime into quarters, using them to rub the salt into the board while squeezing the juice onto the board as you go. Let the board sit for two to three minutes, and then wipe it clean with a damp cloth.

An old toothbrush's bristles lift away stray threads of silk from fresh ears of corn quickly and efficiently.

Chalk is a moisture-absorber so to slow down tarnishing, tie up a few pieces in cheesecloth and store them with your good silver.

Place two small open bottles of disinfectant on your kitchen table or worktop and the flies will stay away.

Cheap cuts of meat can be just as succulent as the finer cuts when cooked slowly in a casserole or slow cooker.

To remove tea stains in a teapot, put four tablespoons of bicarbonate of soda into the pot, fill it the rest of the way with boiling water, and leave the solution overnight. In the morning, rinse it out well and leave it to dry upside-down.

Keep the foil trays from a takeaway and use them to make individual portions of lasagne, pies, etc. which can be stored in the freezer until needed.

Rinsing lettuce leaves in lemon juice will keep them fresh for an extra few days.

Freeze leftover pieces of cake until you have enough to make trifle.

To clear a rusty knife blade use it to chop a fresh onion, chopping with the part that is rusty. The juice from the onion will help loosen the rust and the action of rubbing the now-juiced rust stain against the onion will help rub the rust out. With most rust stains, one onion will remove all of the rust from your knife.

UPCYCLING

Repurpose unwanted/damaged hardback books into cool photo frames. Strip out printed pages at the spine of the book, then strengthen the spine by gluing a cardboard strip on the inside. Cut a photo-sized aperture into both the front and back cover of the remaining jacket, then glue previously cut transparent plastic sheets to overlap the hole. Place a favourite photo onto plastic and tack with sticky tape. Finally, cover the back of your frame with recycled gift wrap.

Shirts and blouses can be given a new lease of life when the collars are worn by unpicking the stitching where the collar is attached to the shirt and turning the collar over, so that the underside of the collar becomes the topside.

Keep old envelopes and bits of paper and staple them together for a telephone pad.

Buy second-hand woollen sweaters or recycle your own that have seen better days. Boil-wash the garments to felt the wool so that the fabric can be cut without it fraying. It can be used to make cosy cushion covers – or let your sewing imagination run wild!

Create unusual wrapping paper by using old magazines, newspapers or out-of-date road map pages to present your gifts.

Make a Valentine's gift by finding a map that shows where you met your beloved. Cut the map into a heart shape with the location in the centre of the heart and attach it to a piece of card and either frame it or make an extra special card.

Pay a visit to your local amenity tip – most will have an area where you can buy unwanted belongings at rock bottom prices – you'll be amazed at what people throw away.

Go for an eco-workout. Take a pair of empty plastic milk cartons (the ones with handles) and fill each with sand or pebbles to make an alternative set of hand weights.

Buy a newspaper brick maker – this is a great way of recycling old newspapers into logs that can be burned on an open fire or a wood-burning stove.

An old Twister game mat makes a great tablecloth for a children's party.

Fold iPod earphones and wires into an old cassette case.

Frugality is the mother of all virtues.

Latin proverb

If you realise that you have enough, you are truly rich.

Lao Tzu

An empty tissue box can be used to store plastic bags tidy and ready for use.

Free hotel shower caps can be used to wrap shoes when travelling, preventing them from dirtying clothes packed in your suitcase.

Store sunglasses inside a winter mitten for protection.

Plastic bottles are ideal for holding indoor and outdoor garden plants. Clean the old 2-litre or gallon-sized bottle and cut in half. Use the bottom half of the bottle and punch holes in it to encourage proper drainage. Add soil and then plant according to plant instructions.

The sleeves of an unwanted jumper can be transformed into a pair of leg warmers by cutting them to the required length and sewing the ends for the feet.

One quick and easy way to revamp a tired-looking piece of wooden furniture is to paint it.

Use pages from old magazines as wrapping paper or to make paper chains at Christmas.

Wash lolly sticks clean when they are finished with and use them as plant markers in the garden.

ENERGY-SAVING TIPS

To reduce ironing time and save energy, put tin foil under the ironing board cover. This will reflect heat up on to the clothes as you iron.

Washing laundry at 30°C instead of 40°C can help save 1.6 billion kilowatt-hours of energy per year.

Water your garden with a watering can – it uses a fraction of the water a hosepipe does, it may be more time-consuming but it's a free workout and therapeutic to pot.

For a chilled drink in the summer, keep a jug of tap water in the fridge. That way, you won't have to run the tap for a long time just to get a cold drink.

For shorter journeys, leave the car at home and cycle or walk. This not only reduces CO_2 emissions and petrol use, but improves fitness and saves money.

Invite your neighbours round to watch the big sports fixtures on your TV for a more sociable and energy-efficient event. Take turns to host.

Car share with Liftshare, National CarShare or easyCar.

Heat from radiators can be partially absorbed by the wall behind them, more so if the radiator is on an outside wall. To reflect heat back from the wall, thus making the radiator more efficient, attach foil with Blu-tack to the wall behind.

Is your journey really necessary?

World War Two slogan

Go by Shanks' pony
Walk short distances
And leave room for those
who have longer journeys

World War Two slogan

Install a water butt to capture rainwater to use in the garden, instead of using tap water. The average UK roof collects 85,000 litres of rainwater each year.

Mulch up your plants – mulches such as pebbles, gravel and chipped bark require low maintenance and are perfect for keeping moisture in the soil, so you need to water less. They also help keep weeds out.

Avoid buying and using disposable plastic or paper cups, plates, cutlery and napkins for picnics. It doesn't take too long to wash up a few plates and the environment will thank you for it.

Use reusable food containers to make your own salads to bring into work – all those plastic salad bowls soon add up to a lot of money and packaging waste, which often can't be recycled.

Save water by replacing damaged washers as soon as the taps start to drip. And remember to turn the tap off while brushing your teeth.

An enormous amount of heat escapes from an open hearth, so when it's not in use, block the opening with fibreboard or a piece of wood.

Wait until you have a full load for the washing machine as this cuts down on wasted electricity.

Turn your heating down by 1ºC to save on your bills.

Rather than using a tumble dryer, dry your washing on a line in the garden. It's free and the washing will smell lovely!

Turn all electrical items off at the plug when not in use. Keeping them on standby uses unnecessary energy.

Use the kettle to boil water for cooking. It's not only more energy-efficient but it will be quicker too.

Save water every time the WC is flushed, by placing a brick or a bottle full of water in the WC cistern. This still provides enough water to flush the toilet but it will not use as much water to refill it. If you can face it apply the adage, 'If it's yellow, let it mellow, if it's brown, flush it down': the water-saving result is obvious.

IN THE GARDEN

An old bathtub, especially a rustic-looking old-fashioned claw-foot tub, or a butler's sink can be filled with soil and plants added, turning it into an unusual planter.

Repair a leaky hosepipe by plugging any puncture holes with toothpicks, saving water and money.

The little plastic cups at the water cooler are ideal for seed-starting pots.

Don't spend money on supporting canes; instead use twigs. They look far less conspicuous and they are free!

Relieve your local garage of old spare tyres to use as planters for potatoes or carrots. Eco-friendly and effective. For carrots, a sandy mix soil in a two deep tyre container will give you lovely and straight crops, free of pests. For potatoes, plant chitted tubers one tyre deep, wait for plants to grow, bank up with soil and add more tyres to the stack (up to about three tyres deep). Once the plants have flowered the potatoes are ready to harvest. Dismantle your tyre stack and harvest the gorgeous treasures from each layer.

Try to water plants in the cool of the evening or very early morning, thus losing less water through evaporation. Direct the flow to the roots, not the leaves, to give your plants maximum benefit.

Treat your veg patch once you have harvested your autumn vegetables; dig out any weeds and turn over with a good dose of compost and manure, then spread old rugs or an unwanted carpet for the winter – you'll have the perfect base to start spring planting the next year.

Make use of holed nylon tights as plant ties – the soft, flexible nature of the fabric will protect new shoots as they grow bigger.

Rake up fallen autumn leaves and stash them into empty bags (e.g. potting compost bags), cover the tops and leave to overwinter; by spring they will have mulched down to make great compost.

Make spring planters. In a good-sized pot, plant layers of bulbs, starting with daffodils/tulips/crocuses – the blooms will appear in early spring and as each variety comes to its end, the next variety will come to life giving you a beautiful showpiece right into early summer.

Keep cut flowers fresh by adding a few drops of bleach to the water in the vase.

To bring on seedlings, take a seed tray, use old newspapers, rolled and fashioned into napkin ring-shaped rounds, or finished toilet roll tubes cut into halves, fill with compost, add seeds according to planting instructions on the packet and water regularly. Once seedlings are ready to be planted out, take the round and transplant directly into the ground. The paper or cardboard will biodegrade and the root system of your seedling will not be destroyed.

Cut lavender at the end of summer, place in paper bags and dry slowly in an airing cupboard or boiler room. The lavender can be used to fill decorative bags that can be hung as air fresheners or moth repellents.

Cut fresh herbs, chop and bag up to place in the freezer. This way, you can have fresh herbs all year round.

Keep a green tree in your heart and perhaps a songbird will come.

Chinese proverb

To forget how to dig the earth and tend the soil is to forget ourselves.

Mahatma Gandhi

Grow peppermint and make a wonderful infusion by cutting the herb and placing the leaves in a cup. Drench with boiling water and steep for five minutes or so. Much nicer than shop-bought teabags.

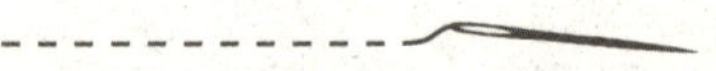

Make sure to invest in a water butt that is connected to a downpipe from a gutter. Rainwater can be preserved in this way and beats using a hosepipe to water plants in the summer by far.

Deal with pest problems organically. For instance, entice slugs away from tempting plants by positioning beer wells nearby – slugs will be lured towards the pungent smell and away from your plants; or crush eggshells and sprinkle around the base of tender plants to avert the destructive munching of slugs and snails.

When you've finished with plastic drinks bottles, make cloches to protect new plants by cutting the bottoms off. Place firmly in the ground to protect the plants from slugs and remove the bottle tops when the plants are more established to allow them to acclimatise.

Use an old broom handle to make your seed trenches by laying the handle along the soil pressing it down firmly, leaving a trench an inch deep.

Brambles may be a little unsightly in a tended garden, but consider keeping an area wild as this will attract beneficial creatures into the garden, such as slow worms and frogs, and the brambles will reward you with blackberries in the summer.

Ash from a bonfire, once cooled, is a rich potash for fruit trees. Spread the ash around the base of fruit trees for a bumper harvest.

Rather than throwing old leather shoes away, bury them in the garden! They will slowly biodegrade, releasing enriching nutrients into the soil.

The unsightly algae that collects on the surface of ponds can be used as an effective alternative to shop-bought fertilisers.

An old Parmesan cheese shaker is perfect for spreading seeds. Simply mix fine seeds with sand and sprinkle where required.

Pick the tops off young nettles and cook for a very tasty vegetable, not dissimilar to spinach.

An old potato peeler makes an excellent job of removing weeds from the lawn.

Retain small yogurt pots and washing balls and balance these upside down on canes planted in the garden. The rattling noise will scare the birds away.

HAVING FUN ON A SHOESTRING

Make sailboats from found or recyclable objects and challenge friends to race them on the local pond or lake.

Try berry-picking in the hedgerows or at pick-your-own farms. Pie-making at home afterwards brings a touch of nostalgia to a late summer's day.

Wild swimming: visit www.outdoorswimmingsociety.com for the best spots and safety advice for swimming outdoors.

Glow-worm spotting: females can be spotted on dry summer nights. They prefer open grasslands and hedges, and thrive in chalk or limestone areas.

Go cycling: the perfect way to explore the world closer to home. Sustrans (www.sustrans.org.uk) has an online map of cycle routes all over Britain.

Orienteering: find courses in your area from www.britishorienteering.co.uk. Older children could set their own course in the city or countryside.

Put on a play with costumes, scenery and props, programmes and tickets.

Hold a 'pets party' and let the children make posters inviting the neighbours.

Have a bake-off with your friends and neighbours and enjoy the results at the end of it.

Skipping: this is fun for one child or a group of children. Learn a few songs and games to play for group skipping, and try to see how many jumps each person can make before making a mistake.

Happiness is making the most of what you have.

Rosamunde Pilcher

It is better to have enough ideas for some of them to be wrong, than to be always right by having no ideas at all.

Edward de Bono

Puddle jumping: nothing is more fun than playing outside when it's raining. Summer rainstorms don't always mean heading inside – put on bathing suits and wellies and stomp in the puddles!

Many vegetables and herbs can be grown indoors or out using containers. Let your children pick some varieties to grow and tend to them throughout the summer. It may tempt them to eat vegetables that they'd normally decline.

Set plastic cups on the top of a fence or wall as targets, and squirt them off with water guns or plastic water bottles. Score points by writing on the plastic cups or just see who's the fastest to knock over the cups.

Camp out in the back garden. Pitch up the tent, build a fire (if local laws allow), toast marshmallows and be prepared for an early morning wake-up.

Fill some balloons with water and have water balloon fun – start kids standing close together and each time the balloon is caught without breaking everyone takes a step back!

Try oversized painting – tape several large sheets of paper together and place them on the patio or lawn. Fill a few containers with different colours of poster paints. Use whatever is lying around to apply the paint: cotton reels, brushes, sponges, drinking straws…

For a scavenger hunt create a list of twenty or more things that can be found naturally outside in your area, things like pine cones, acorns, feathers, specific flowers, nuts, etc. Send the children on a hunt to try to collect one of each item on the list. This can be done as a group effort, or each child can compete with the other to see who can find the most objects, the fastest.

Have fun washing the family car (and each other) using the hose, a bucket, soap and some sponges.

Let the children create an amazing obstacle course in the back garden, from toys, bikes, and other things that they find. Just keep an eye on them so they aren't doing anything that would be unsafe.

Go to a car boot sale. Give each child a few pounds and allow them to make purchases. Even better, have a clear-out and run your own car boot sale.

Go fishing: borrow fishing equipment if you don't have any and spend the day fishing in a river, lake or pond.

Make a piñata from papier mâché. Mix water and flour in a bowl to create a paste. Cut up strips of newspapers and stick layers over an inflated balloon. Just remember it takes several days for it to dry before you can add small treats, and paint and decorate it.

Make puppets using socks and craft supplies from around the house. Then put on a puppet show.

If you have a digital camera, consider letting the children take photos throughout the summer or give them a few disposable cameras for them to use. Using your craft supplies, create mini-scrapbooks of what the kids did over their summer holidays or any special occasion.

Create your own board game with cardboard, crayons and other objects – then play it! The real fun is the creation of the game itself, but the game can be saved for future playtimes as well.

If you live near a sandy beach, have a sand sculpture or sand castle competition, or make dribble castles using slopping sand and water, or sketch out a hopscotch grid and use a pebble as a marker – endless hours of free entertainment.

FOOD AND DRINK

Buy cauliflowers with all their leaves still on and leave them on while storing, as this stops them going brown.

If there is uneaten Stilton cheese at Christmas, it can be frozen and later used up in a homemade celery soup.

One brown banana left in the fruit bowl can be added to a curry. It works well with vegetables or lentils and adds fruitiness without being a definite taste.

To avoid soggy, unused vegetables in the fridge, peel and chop carrots, onions, etc., bag them and freeze. When needed, just take out as much as is needed and reseal.

Put a piece of scrap paper in with the vegetables in the fridge drawer. Any moisture goes in the paper not the vegetables or salad.

Add stale or leftover breakfast cereal crumbs from the bottom of the cereal box to the ingredients in the bread maker, while reducing the amount of flour accordingly. This adds texture to the bread, and even sweet breakfast cereal doesn't make the bread sweet.

To extract the most juice from a lemon, roll it up and down the worktop, pressing hard.

Freshly squeezed lemon juice can be frozen in ice cube moulds to use another time – add to water to give a refreshing zing.

If you are only eating
what you need
and not what you like and
as much as you like,
then you are helping to
win the war.

Lord Woolton,
broadcast during World War Two

Beware of little expenses; a small leak will sink a great ship.

Benjamin Franklin

Pesto can be frozen in teaspoonfuls in an airtight container. When it's needed, defrost in a dish.

When baking, if you find you are short of eggs, substitute 1 tablespoon of white vinegar per egg – the results in cakes and muffins are impressive.

Make mince pies in early December and freeze uncooked in their baking tins until solid. They can then be packed in boxes and baked a few at a time when needed.

Fresh or long-life semi-skimmed milk can be frozen when too much has been bought and the family are away for a few days. It also means that there is always milk for a cup of tea on arrival home to an otherwise empty fridge.

Be inventive with leftovers – try to avoid throwing food away: boil up a chicken carcass to make a tasty soup stock with a few carrots, an onion, a leek, some celery; mash potatoes and mix with leftover vegetables from a Sunday roast to make a comfort food 'bubble and squeak'; use leftover potatoes and veg to create a fabulous frittata.

Mix yogurt with any overripe fruit such as banana and strawberries and pour into lolly moulds and freeze.

Naan bread makes a great ready-made pizza base and is often on bulk buy offers. Spread liberally with pizza sauce and any topping. Freeze for another day.

Slice fresh bagels and freeze in plastic bags. When required, take them out of the freezer bags and put them directly in the toaster.

An iceberg lettuce can be broken up and stored in the fridge in a bowl of cold water allowing it to stay fresh and crispy for much longer than normal.

Wrap celery in foil and store in the fridge to keep it fresher for longer.

If apples have bruised areas, simply cut off and grate the remaining apple into salads or cut into wedges and eat as a snack.

Better pot-luck with
Churchill today
Than humble pie under
Hitler tomorrow
Don't waste food!

World War Two slogan

It is thrifty to prepare today for the wants of tomorrow.

Aesop

If bananas have been bought in a bag they will stay firmer and look better for at least a few days longer if they remain in the bag.

When making bolognese sauce or shepherd's pie, add a finely grated carrot and a finely grated courgette to the mix at the same time as the mince to bulk it out and increase vegetable intake.

Hold a day-old loaf of bread briefly under a running cold tap. After a good shake, pop in a hot oven for about ten minutes and it will be as soft and crusty as freshly baked bread.

To make an instant crouton mix, cut any leftover bread into cubes, toss in olive oil and a little garlic, herbs and chilli powder, freeze on a tray and transfer into bags or boxes when frozen. These can then be shallow fried or baked in the oven and added to any soup or salad.

Mix leftover pesto with butter and freeze in individual portions. The pesto butter can then be used on steak, chicken, lamb, etc.

Instead of buying bottles of mineral water buy a reusable water bottle. Place an inspirational sticker or image onto it, or even write on it with a permanent marker.

Iced tea requires only one-half as much sugar if sweetened when hot than when cold.

Milk frequently sticks to the pan when it is being boiled. To prevent this, rinse the pan in hot water before heating.

To bake a potato in half the usual time, stick a metal skewer lengthways through the centre of the potato.

To keep the fizz in an unfinished canned drink, put the end of a teaspoon in the can and the next day it will still be fizzy.

DIY

A plastic bag can be tightly secured with a rubber band to keep a brush (or roller) moist for a day or two in between painting sessions.

When painting ceilings and walls, add the roller to a pole. It gives an even pressure and a whole room can be painted with very little effort.

A great method of removing wall paper is to make a mixture of warm water, a detergent such as washing-up liquid and something to thicken the mixture (wall paper adhesive is ideal). Mix the warm water, washing-up liquid and wallpaper paste; do not mix too much wallpaper paste as it will make the liquid too thick. Soak for 20 minutes then remove with a scraper.

Don't throw old tins of paint away as there may be times in the future when there is a need to touch-up scuffed areas.

To clean emulsion paint off a paintbrush, rinse under a running tap until the water runs clear. Remove any remaining water by making brushstrokes on some newspaper. If the paintbrush isn't going to be used for a while, wrap it in some paper before putting it away.

If drilling on tiles or hard walls, the drill tip can be prone to slipping, so to prevent this simply stick on some masking tape before marking the spot.

If using a drill without a depth guide on it, use a piece of tape wrapped round the drill bit to show how deep it needs to go.

When drilling into walls (especially brick) a lot of dust will come out and make a mess. So fold a large Post-it note in to a V-shape and stick it directly under the place to be drilled. The dust falls into the Post-it.

Onions are high in sulphur so have a detoxifying effect. Put half an onion in a room when painting to diminish the ill effects from the paint fumes.

Decant paint into a small bowl when painting with a paintbrush, as this will keep the can free of the impurities (dust, wood particles, etc.) that your brush may pick up as you work.

I went to the hardware store and bought some used paint. It was in the shape of a house.

Steven Wright

Use it up, wear it out, make it do, or do without.

New England proverb

Hard paintbrushes can be rejuvenated – after a spell in hot vinegar, comb the bristles with a fork and keep in shape with an elastic band until dry.

On first opening a new tin of paint, tie a piece of string tightly between the two rivets where the handle connects. This provides a place to wipe the brush and rest it without getting paint all over the tin.

To prevent a messy paint roller tray, wrap the roller tray in cling-film and just roll up the cling-film and throw it away afterwards.

To rejuvenate masking tape, put the tape in a microwave oven with a glass of water. Set the oven on full for about a minute. Switch off and check the tape has become quite warm, though not overheated. The tape will now peel off just as it did when new.

To prevent rusty tools in the toolbox, pop in some silica packets (make use of the little white packets found in lots of packaging). They help absorb damp and prevent metal from rusting.

Sugar soap used for preparing walls and furniture before painting is also good for removing gloss paint splashes from doors and window ledges. It just comes off with a rub and a cloth.

When painting, particularly when using gloss paint, smear Vaseline or a similar oily substance over your hands to make them much easier to wash afterwards.

When using gloss paint, after a while it starts to go thick and is harder to paint with. Add a generous squirt of washing-up liquid to the paint. Give it a good stir and it will go further, spread better and will not leave brush marks.

To paint railings, use a car-cleaning mitten. Put paint on the mitten, take off the surplus and then grip the railing with the mitt and run your hand up and down. Easy, quick and much less tedious than using a brush.

If painting pipes which are fixed to a wall, cut out a piece of cardboard, place this behind the pipes to be painted and then paint in the usual way. This will prevent any paint getting onto the wall behind.

To paint a wall with emulsion but with no brush or roller, a normal house sponge can be used instead.

When using a ladder against painted masonry, put old socks over the end of the ladder to prevent it damaging the stonework.

When peeling paper off a ceiling, first put a bin liner over the back of the step ladder into which the paper can be placed as soon as it is removed. This saves a lot of cleaning up at the end of the day.

If sash windows are stiff to open and shut, put candle wax or soap down the side runners.

Cat litter can be used for absorbing oil spills in garages etc. Dilute any spills with paint thinner or white spirit, sprinkle with cat litter and sweep up when the liquid has been absorbed.

If you have wallpaper left over after a decorating project, use as linings for drawers or as wrapping paper.

BAKE FOR BRITAIN

£4.99

Hardback

ISBN: 978-1-84953-267-9

'Come along inside... We'll see if tea and buns can make the world a better place.'

Kenneth Grahame

TASTY ADVICE FOR BRITISH BAKERS

Sumptuous scones with jam and clotted cream, lemon drizzle cake, Victoria sponge and brandy snaps – just a few of the sweet treats that get British taste buds tingling. So put on your apron, dig out the mixing bowl and start the oven because it's time to go baking mad.

Here's a book packed with recipes and quotations to help you bake your country proud.

DIG FOR VICTORY

£4.99

Hardback

ISBN: 978-1-84953-276-1

'It's difficult to think anything but pleasant thoughts while eating a home-grown tomato.'

Lewis Grizzard

WISE WORDS FOR GARDENERS

The World War Two slogan is still pertinent in these thrifty times as more people than ever are turning to self-sufficiency and growing their own fruit and vegetables. This little compendium is packed with tips and hints on how to make the most of your garden along with witty quotations to help you to dig for victory.

MAKE DO AND MEND

MAKE DO AND MEND

MAKE DO AND MEND

MAKE DO AND MEND

MAKE DO AND MEND

MAKE DO AND MEND

MAKE DO AND MEND

MAKE DO AND MEND

MAKE DO AND MEND

MAKE DO AND MEND

MAKE DO AND MEND

MAKE DO AND MEND

MAKE MAKE MAKE
DO DO DO
AND AND AND
MEND MEND MEND M

MAKE MAKE MAKE M
DO DO DO
AND AND AND A
END MEND MEND ME

MAKE MAKE MAKE
DO DO DO
AND AND AND
MEND MEND MEND M

MAKE MAKE MAKE M
DO DO DO
AND AND AND A
END MEND MEND ME